CROCHET  EVERYDAY

Publications International, Ltd.

Consulting by Heidi Beazley

Written by Beth Taylor

Photo styling by Jessi LeDonne and Amy Stark

Photography by Christopher Hiltz, except pages 4, 21, and 30 from Shutterstock.com

Crochet symbols and abbreviations from Craft Yarn Council's www.YarnStandards.com

Louis Weber, CEO
Publications International, Ltd.
8140 Lehigh Avenue
Morton Grove, IL 60053

ISBN: 978-1-68022-806-9

Manufactured in China.

8 7 6 5 4 3 2 1

TABLE OF CONTENTS

STITCH VARIATIONS

Double Herringbone
(HBdc)

The double herringbone stitch is basically a modified double crochet stitch. To make a double herringbone stitch, start with a foundation chain.

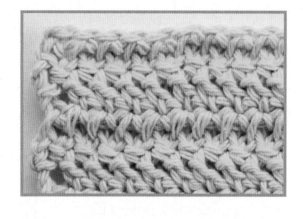

1 Yarn over and insert your hook into the third chain from your hook. There are 3 loops on your hook.

2 Yarn over and draw the yarn through the first 2 loops on your hook. There are 2 loops on your hook.

3 Yarn over and draw the yarn through the first loop on your hook. There are still 2 loops on your hook.

4 Yarn over and draw the yarn through both loops on your hook. You will have 1 loop on your hook when your first HBdc stitch is complete.

5 Continue to the end of the row. Chain 3 for the turning chain. Turn your work so the opposite side faces you. Skip the 3 turning chains and the first stitch. Yarn over and insert your hook into the next stitch.

Repeat steps 2–5 to continue the pattern.

Clusters (CL)

You make clusters by combining stitches together into the same stitch or space.

To make cluster stitches using single crochet, start with a foundation chain that has a multiple of 2 chains, plus 1.

Tip: **How to single crochet 2 together using 2 chain spaces:**

1. Insert your hook into the chain space to be worked.
2. Yarn over and draw the yarn through the space. You will have 2 loops on your hook.
3. Insert your hook into the next chain space.
4. Yarn over and draw the yarn through the space. There will be 3 loops on your hook.
5. Yarn over and draw the yarn through all 3 loops on your hook. There will be 1 loop left on your hook.

these are the chain spaces

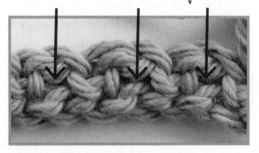

Row 1:

In the second chain from your hook, work 1 single crochet stitch.

Chain 1. Skip 1 chain and work 1 single crochet into the next chain. Repeat step 2 across the row. Chain 1 for the turning chain.

Row 2:

Turn your work so that the opposite side faces you. Work 1 single crochet into the first stitch of the row. Chain 1.

Following the tip instructions, single crochet 2 together (sc2tog), working into the next 2 chain spaces. Chain 1 when you're finished.

work back into this chain space

Insert your hook back into the chain space you just worked in. Single crochet 2 together using this chain space and the next. Chain 1.

Repeat step 3 across the row, ending the row with 1 single crochet in the last stitch. Chain 1 for the turning chain and turn your work so that the opposite side faces you.

Row 3:

1. Work 1 single crochet into the first stitch.

2. Chain 1.

3. Skip 1 chain and work 1 single crochet into the next stitch.

4. Repeat steps 2–3 across the row.

Repeat rows 2–3 to continue the pattern.

V-Stitch

The V-stitch makes a series of interlocking Vs. This stitch works up quickly and is great for making afghans.

To make V-stitches using double crochet, start with a foundation chain that has a multiple of 3 chains, plus 7.

Row 1:

1 Work 1 double crochet into the fourth chain from your hook. Chain 1.

2 Skip 1 chain stitch and work 1 double crochet into the next chain. Chain 1.

3 Work 1 double crochet into the very same chain. You will have 1 loop on your hook when your first V-stitch is complete.

4 Skip 2 chains and work 1 double crochet into the next chain. Chain 1. Work 1 double crochet into the very same stitch.

5

Repeat step 4 across the row until you have 4 chains left. Chain 1.

6

Skip 2 chains. Work 1 double crochet into each of the last 2 chains to end the row.

7

At the end of the row, chain 3 for the turning chain. Turn your work so the opposite side faces you.

Tip: A chain-1 space is the space created by the chain 1 between the 2 double crochet stitches. It looks like the center of a V.

this is a chain-1 space →

Row 2:

1

The turning chain counts as the first double crochet in this row. Work 1 double crochet into the next stitch and chain 1.

2

Work 1 V-stitch into each chain-1 space (center of each V) across the row until you have 1 chain space and 2 double crochet stitches left.

3 When you have 1 chain space and 2 double crochet stitches left, chain 1 and skip the chain-1 space. Work 1 double crochet into each of the last 2 double crochet stitches to end the row. Chain 3 for the turning chain and turn.

Repeat row 2 to continue the pattern.

Popcorns (pc)

The popcorn stitch works several stitches into the same space, resulting in a "puffed" pattern and texture.

To make a popcorn using single and double crochet, start with a foundation chain that has a multiple of 3 chain stitches.

Row 1:

Work 1 single crochet into the second chain from your hook.

Finish the row with single crochet stitches. Chain 1 for the turning chain.

Row 2:

Turn your work so the opposite side faces you. Work a single crochet into each of the next 2 stitches.

In the next stitch, work 5 double crochets into the same stitch. Drop the loop you created by removing your hook.

3

Insert your hook under the top 2 loops of the first double crochet of the group.

4

Grab the dropped loop with your hook and draw the yarn through the stitch. Add a chain stitch to complete your first popcorn stitch. You will have 1 loop on your hook.

5

Work 1 single crochet into each of the next 3 stitches.

6

Continue to the end of the row, alternating between the popcorn stitch and the single crochet stitches. At the end of row, chain 1 for the turning chain.

Row 3:

1

Turn your work so the opposite side faces you. Work 1 single crochet stitch into each stitch across the row.

Tip: For rows of staggered popcorn stitches like in our example swatch, reduce the number of single crochet stitches at the beginning of every other popcorn row. Then complete the popcorn rows as usual.

Repeat rows 2–3 to continue the pattern.

Crossed Stitches

Crossed stitches cross back over the front of previous stitches to form a unique X pattern. Double and treble crochet are the most common stitches used to cross.

To make crossed stitches using double crochet, start with a foundation chain that has a multiple of 2 chains.

Row 1:

In the fifth chain from your hook, work 1 double crochet. There is 1 loop on your hook.

Crossing over the front of the double crochet you just made, work 1 double crochet into the last skipped chain.

You will have 1 loop on your hook when your first pair of crossed stitches is complete.

Chain 1. Skip 1 chain and work 1 double crochet into the next chain after that.

5 Crossing over the front of the double crochet you just made, work 1 double crochet into the last skipped chain.

6 Repeat steps 4–5 across the row. At the end of the row, work 1 double crochet into the last chain.

7 Chain 3 for the turning chain and turn your work so that the opposite side faces you.

Tip: How to make crossed treble stitches:

1. Start with an odd number foundation chain.

2. In the sixth chain from your hook, work 1 treble crochet stitch.

3. Follow steps 2–6, replacing double crochet with treble crochet stitches.

4. Chain 4 for the turning chain and turn.

Row 2:

1. Skip the first 2 stitches and work 1 double crochet into the next double crochet stitch.

2. Crossing over the front of the double crochet you just made, work 1 double crochet into the last skipped stitch.

3. Chain 1. Skip the next double crochet stitch and work 1 double crochet into the last skipped stitch.

4. Repeat step 3 until the last stitch of the row. Work 1 double crochet into the last stitch.

5. Chain 3 and turn.

Repeat row 2 to continue the pattern.

Bobbles (bo)

Bobbles work multiple stitches together into 1 stitch or space.

This bobble uses single and double crochet. Start with a foundation chain that has any odd number of chains.

Row 1:

1 In the 2nd chain from your hook, work 1 single crochet stitch.

2 Chain 1. Skip 1 chain and work 1 single crochet stitch into the next chain. Repeat step 2 across the row.

3 At the end of the row, chain 3 for the turning chain and turn your work so that the opposite side faces you.

Row 2:

1 Skip the first stitch. (The turning chain counts as the first double crochet in this row.)

Row 2 (continued):

In the next chain space, double crochet 5 together (dc5tog) following the tip instructions.

Tip: How to double crochet 5 together:

1. Yarn over. Insert your hook into the chain space.

2. Yarn over and draw the yarn through the space.

3. Yarn over and draw the yarn through the first 2 loops on your hook.

4. Repeat steps 1–3, inserting your hook into the same chain space, until you have 6 loops on your hook. Each time you repeat this process, you will add another loop to your hook.

On your final bobble, yarn over and draw the yarn through all 6 loops on your hook. (You will have 1 loop on your hook when your 5 double crochets are complete.)

Make 1 chain stitch to secure and complete the bobble.

Repeat steps 2–4 across the row, ending with 1 double crochet in the last single crochet of the row. Chain 1 for the turning chain and turn your work.

Row 3:

1. Work 1 single crochet into the first stitch.

2. Chain 1. Skip 1 chain and work 1 single crochet into the next stitch.

3. Repeat step 2 across the row.

Repeat rows 2–3 to continue the pattern.

Shell Stitch

Shells are created by working several stitches into the same stitch or space. They are also called fan stitches.

To make shell stitches using single and double crochet, start with a foundation chain that has a multiple of 4 chains, plus 1.

Row 1:

In the fifth chain from your hook, work 4 double crochet stitches.

Skip the next 3 chains and work 4 double crochet stitches into the next chain.

Repeat step 2 across the row until there are 4 chains left. Skip 3 chains and work 2 double crochet stitches into the last chain. Chain 1 for the turning chain and turn your work so that the opposite side faces you.

Row 2:

Work 1 single crochet into each of the double crochet stitches from the previous row. Chain 3 for the turning chain and turn your work so that the opposite side faces you.

Row 3:

1. Work 1 double crochet into the first stitch. Skip 3 stitches.

2. Work 4 double crochets into the next single crochet stitch. Skip the next 3 single crochet stitches.

3. Repeat step 2 across the row until there are 2 stitches left.

4. Skip the next single crochet stitch and work 1 double crochet into the last stitch.

5. Chain 1 for the turning chain and turn your work so that the opposite side faces you.

Row 4:

1. Work 1 single crochet into the next double crochet.

2. Continue working 1 single crochet into each double crochet stitch across the row.

3. Work 1 single crochet stitch into the top of the turning chain from the previous row.

4. Chain 3 for the turning chain and turn your work so that the opposite side faces you.

Row 5:

1. Skip the first 2 single crochet stitches.

2. Work 4 double crochet stitches into the next single crochet.

3. Skip the next 3 single crochets.

4. Repeat steps 2–3 across the row until there are 2 stitches left.

5. Skip the next stitch and work 1 double crochet stitch into the last stitch of the previous row.

6. Chain 1 for the turning chain and turn your work so that the opposite side faces you.

Repeat rows 4–5 to continue the pattern.

Basketweave

This basketweave uses alternating front post double crochet (FPdc) and back post double crochet (BPdc) stitches. Post stitches are sometimes called raised stitches.

Start with a foundation chain that has a multiple of 6 chains, plus 4.

Front & Back Posts:

Instead of inserting your hook into a stitch or space, you insert it around the front or back of a post. The stitches are worked the same as usual. The only difference is where your hook is inserted.

posts

Front Posts:
Insert your hook under the post from the front side.

Back Posts:
Insert your hook under the post from the back side.

Row 1:

In the 4th chain from your hook, work 1 double crochet. Continue across the row, working 1 double crochet into each chain.

Chain 2 for the turning chain and turn your work so that the opposite side faces you.

Row 2:

1 Work 1 double crochet around the 2nd front post of the previous row (FPdc). To do this, yarn over (because you are doing a double crochet) and insert your hook under the 2nd post. Finish your double crochet stitch as usual.

2 Work a FPdc stitch into the next 2 posts so there are a total of 3.

3 Work 1 double crochet around the next back post (BPdc). To do this, yarn over (because you are doing a double crochet) and insert your hook, from the back side, under the next post. Finish your double crochet stitch as usual.

4 Work a BPdc stitch into the next 2 posts so there are a total of 3.

5 Continue across the row, alternating 3 FPdc stitches with 3 BPdc stitches. Finish the row by working 1 double crochet into the top chain of the turning chain.

6 Chain 2 for the turning chain and turn your work so that the opposite side faces you.

Row 3:

Repeat row 2, alternating 3 FPdc stitches with 3 BPdc stitches across the row. Work 1 double crochet into the top of the turning chain. Chain 2 and turn.

Row 4:

Work 1 BPdc stitch around the 2nd post. Work 1 BPdc stitch around the next 2 posts for a total of 3 BPdc stitches.

Work 3 FPdc stitches around the next 3 posts. Continue across the row, alternating 3 BPdc stitches with 3 FPdc stitches.

3. Work 1 double crochet into the top of the last turning chain.

4. Chain 2 for the turning chain and turn your work so that the opposite side faces you.

Row 5:

1. Repeat row 4, alternating 3 BPdc stitches with 3 FPdc stitches across the row. Work 1 double crochet into the top of the turning chain. Chain 2 and turn.

Repeat rows 2–5 to continue the pattern.

FINISHING TECHNIQUES

Edging Techniques

There are many different edging techniques, which can be crocheted or sewn.
Each technique will give your piece a finished and unique look. Here are a few examples.

Shell Stitch Edge

The shells in this example are made from 5 double crochet stitches into the same single crochet stitch. Start with a row of single crochet around the edge of your piece.

1 Insert your hook into the single crochet stitch in the upper right-hand corner and secure the yarn with a slip stitch. Chain 3.

2 In the next stitch, work 2 double crochets.

3 Chain 1. Skip 1 stitch and work 1 single crochet into the next stitch.

4 Chain 1. Skip 1 stitch and work 5 double crochets into the next stitch. Your first 5-dc shell is complete.

5 Repeat steps 2–4 around your entire piece. End with 3 more double crochets in the same stitch into which you worked the 2 double crochets in step 2 to complete the 5-dc shell.

Picot
Stitch Edge

Picot edges can either be made small or large. They can be worked into stitches or spaces and can be added to any row of stitches. Here picots are added to rows of single crochet.

Small picot

Large picot

Small Picot

1 Insert your hook anywhere along the edge and join your edging yarn with a slip stitch.

2 Chain 3. Insert your hook into the third chain from your hook. Yarn over and draw the yarn through both loops to complete 1 small picot.

3 Work 1 single crochet into each of the next 3 stitches.

4 Alternate 1 small picot with 3 single crochet stitches around the edges.

Large Picot

1. Insert your hook anywhere along the edge and join your edging yarn with a slip stitch.

2. Chain 5. Insert your hook into the fifth chain from your hook. Yarn over and draw the yarn through both loops to complete 1 large picot.

3. Work 1 single crochet into each of the next 3 stitches.

4. Alternate 1 large picot with 3 single crochet stitches around the edges.

Crab Stitch Edge

Crab stitch is also called reverse single crochet. Start with a row of single crochet along the edge.

1 Secure the new yarn with a slip stitch in the top left-hand corner.

2 Insert your hook into the same stitch you just worked into.

3 Yarn over and draw the yarn through the stitch (the first loop on your hook). There are 2 loops on your hook.

4 Yarn over again and draw the yarn through both loops on your hook. You will have 1 loop on your hook when your first crab stitch is complete.

5 Repeat steps 2–4 across the edge, working 1 crab stitch into each single crochet to the right.

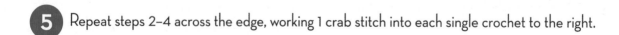

Tip: To continue the edging around a corner, work multiple crab stitches into the same corner stitch.

Blanket Stitch Edge

The blanket stitch is sewn rather than crocheted. It lies flat and can help disguise uneven edges.

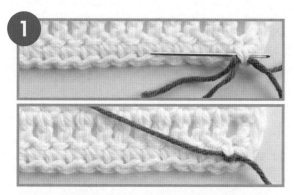

1 Thread the yarn through the large eye of a tapestry needle. With the wrong side facing up, secure the yarn to the bottom right-hand side of the crochet piece.

2 Flip the crochet piece so the right side is facing up. Draw the needle from back to front through the bottom left-hand side.

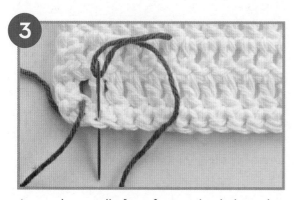

3 Insert the needle from front to back through the next small space on the edge.

4 Pull the needle through, going over the loop that was created. You have completed 1 blanket stitch.

5 Continue across the edge, working blanket stitches into the spaces between stitches.

Tip: To continue the edging around a corner, work multiple blanket stitches into the same corner space.

Joining Pieces Together

There are many techniques for joining pieces together, including both crochet and sewing methods. Some methods create a more bulky seam and will be more sturdy. Other methods are less bulky, but might be more delicate. Use the same yarn from your project to help disguise the seams. Using a different color yarn makes seams more obvious, but can add more detail to your project.

Single Crochet Join

To join crochet pieces together with single crochet, start by placing the pieces with right sides together and stitches or rows lined up.

Tip: The only difference between a regular row of single crochet stitches and a single crochet join is that you will be working each stitch in both pieces.

| Front side | Back side |

1 Insert your hook from front to back under the first pair of stitches on both pieces. Make a slip knot and attach it to the end of your hook.

2 Draw the slip knot through both pieces, letting the knot catch on the back. Yarn over and draw through the loop on your hook. Yarn over again and draw through both loops on your hook.

3 Insert your hook from front to back under the next pair of stitches and work a single crochet stitch.

4 Repeat step 3 across the seam, working 1 single crochet in each pair of stitches. When complete, fasten off and weave in yarn tails.

Slip Stitch Join

To join crochet pieces with slip stitch, start by placing the pieces with right sides together and stitches or rows lined up.

Tip: To make the slip stitch seam less bulky, try only working through 1 loop of each stitch.

1 Insert your hook from front to back under the first corresponding pair of stitches of both pieces on the right. Make a slip knot and attach it to the end of your hook.

2 Draw the slip knot through both pieces. The knot will catch on the back. Yarn over and draw the yarn through the loop on your hook.

3 Insert your hook from front to back under the next pair of corresponding stitches on the left. Yarn over and draw the yarn through both loops on your hook. You will have 1 loop on your hook when your first slip stitch is complete.

4 Repeat step 3 across the seam. When complete, fasten off and weave in yarn tails.

Ladder Stitch Join

The ladder stitch creates seams that are flat and nearly invisible (as long as you use the same color yarn).

To join 2 crochet pieces with ladder stitch, start by placing the pieces with right sides together and stitches or rows lined up.

1

On the top crochet piece, insert your threaded tapestry needle through the outside loop of the bottom left-hand stitch, and then through the same outside loop on the bottom piece.

2

Working in the opposite direction as your last stitch, bring your needle through only the outside loops of the next stitches above on both crochet pieces.

3

Repeat step 2 up the seam. Pull both yarn tails to tighten and weave in the tails.

Backstitch Join

The backstitch is a sewing method you can use to join crochet pieces together. It is extra strong, but bulky.

To join 2 crochet pieces with backstitch, start by placing the pieces with right sides together and stitches or rows lined up. Cut a piece of matching yarn to sew with. A piece too long will be difficult to work with.

Front side

Back side

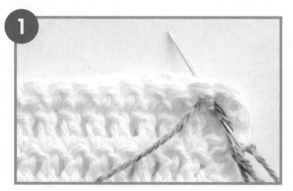

Using a threaded tapestry needle, secure the yarn close to the top right edge. Insert the needle from front to back through both pieces in the first stitch.

From back to front, bring the needle through the next stitch on the left. Draw the yarn through. From front to back, insert the needle into the first stitch and draw through.

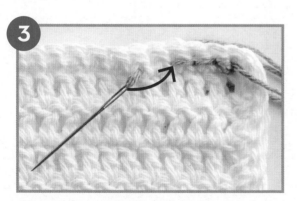

Skip the first stitch on the left. From back to front, bring the needle through the next stitch. Draw the yarn through. From front to back, insert the needle into the previous stitch and draw through.

4 Repeat step 3 across the seam. When complete, fasten off and weave in the yarn tails.

Tip: Match the size of your backstiches to the size of the crochet stitches in your piece.

Abbreviations & Symbols

Crochet patterns often use abbreviations and symbols as shorthand to represent frequently used stitches and techniques. Use the guide below as you start to follow patterns using shorthand.

Abbreviations

alt	alternate
approx	approximately
beg	begin/beginning
bet	between
BL	back loop(s)
bo	bobble
BP	back post
BPdc	back post double crochet
BPsc	back post single crochet
BPtr	back post treble crochet
CC	contrasting color
ch	chain(s)
ch-sp	chain space
CL	cluster
cm	centimeter(s)
cont	continue
dc	double crochet
dec	decrease(s)/decreasing
dtr	double treble
edc	extended double crochet
ehdc	extended half double crochet
esc	extended single crochet
FL	front loop(s)
FP	front post
FPdc	front post double crochet
FPtr	front post treble crochet
hdc	half double crochet
hk	hook
inc	increase(s)/increasing
lp(s)	loop(s)
MC	main color
mm	millimeter(s)

p	picot
pc	popcorn
pat(s)	pattern(s)
pm	place marker
prev	previous
rem	remain/remaining
rep	repeat(s)
rnd(s)	round(s)
RS	right side
sc	single crochet
sl st	slip stitch
sk	skip
sp(s)	space(s)
st(s)	stitch(es)
tch	turning chain
tog	together
tr	treble crochet
WS	wrong side
yd(s)	yard(s)
yo	yarn over
"	inch(es)
[ ]	work instructions within brackets as many times as directed
( )	work instructions within parentheses as many times as directed
*	repeat the instructions following the single asterisk as directed
**	repeat the instructions between asterisks as many times as directed or repeat from a given set of instructions

Symbols

⬯	chain
•	slip stitch
X or †	single crochet
T	half double crochet
T	double crochet
T	treble crochet
⋏	sc2tog
⋏	sc3tog
人	dc2tog
人	dc3tog
⬯	3-dc cluster
⬯	3-hdc cluster/ puff st/bobble
⬯	5-dc popcorn
⬯	5-dc shell
⬯	ch-3 picot
⬯	front post dc
⬯	back post dc
⌒	worked in back loop only**
⌣	worked in front loop only**

**Symbol appears at base of stitch being worked.

EVERYDAY CROCHET PATTERNS

Cord Cover

Skill Level

BEGINNER

Materials

SUPER FINE
1

Hook: 3.5 mm/U.S. E-4
Other: Any cords or headphones to cover, yarn needle

Stitches Used

Single crochet (sc)
Slip stitch (sl st)

Instructions

Make a slip knot on your hook. Holding the yarn tail under the cord, make a sc around the cord and tail.

Continue making sc sts around cord until you reach end. (If the cord splits, or if you reach microphone, button, or volume controls, stop. Fasten off and restart on the other side.)

Fasten off when done covering cord and weave in ends.

Tip: When working your sc stitches around the cord, put your hook under the cord as if you were working into a stitch. Once under the cord, yarn over and complete your sc as usual. Every so often, push your stitches together along the cord to make sure there are no gaps.

Basket

Hook: 8 mm/U.S. L-11
Other: Yarn needle

Skill Level

EASY

Materials

SUPER BULKY
6 4 skeins

Stitches Used

Chain stitch (ch)
Double crochet (dc)
Single crochet (sc)
Slip stitch (sl st)

Instructions

This basket is worked with 2 strands of yarn held together throughout. For a smaller basket, use fewer chains for the bottom. For a larger basket, use more chains for the bottom.

Basket Bottom

With 2 strands of yarn, ch 25.

Row 1: Skip first ch, sc in each st across row.

Rows 2–18: Ch 1, turn, sc in each st across row.

Basket Sides

You will now work in rounds, placing sts around the rectangular base you just made.

Round 1: Ch 2, dc around basket bottom, going through just the back loop only of st. (This makes the turning edge.) Sl st to beginning ch.

Rounds 2–5: Ch 2, dc in each st around, going through both loops of st. Sl st to beginning ch.

Basket Handles

Round 1: Ch 2, dc in each st until on the first short side of basket. Dc until there are 8 sts evenly in center of short edge, ch 9 sts, skip next 8 sts, dc in each st again until at opposite short side of the basket. Dc in each st until there are 8 sts evenly in center of opposite short edge, ch 9 sts, skip next 8 sts, dc in the remaining sts left, sl st to beginning ch.

Round 2: Ch 2, dc in each st (including ch sts), sl st to beginning ch. Fasten off and weave in ends.

Tip: This simple basket is perfect for stashing all of your stuff! Try using it to store your yarn and other craft supplies.

Hanging Organizer

Skill Level

EASY

Materials

 1 large skein (220 yards)

Hook: 6.5 mm/U.S. K-10.5

Other: 3 large buttons, hanger, yarn needle

Stitches Used

Chain stitch (ch)
Half double crochet (hdc)
Single crochet (sc)

Instructions

This crocheted organizer is intended to hang from 3 button tabs that are folded over a hanger bar. The hanging organizer is approximately 12.5" wide and 15" high. It can also be adjusted to any size by increasing or decreasing the starting chain.

Base

Ch 27.

Row 1: Hdc in 3rd ch from hook and in each ch st across.

Rows 2–21: Ch 2, turn, hdc in each stitch across.

First Button Tab

Row 22: Hdc in next 5 stitches, ch 2, turn.

Rows 23–24: Repeat row 22.

Row 25: Hdc in next 2 stitches, ch 1, hdc in last 2 stitches, ch 1, turn.

Row 26: Sc in next 2 stitches, sc in the ch-1 sp, sc in the last 2 stitches.

Fasten off.

Tip: How to half double crochet
Yarn over and insert hook into the indicated chain or stitch. (You will have 3 loops on your hook.) Yarn over and draw through the first loop on your hook. (You will have 3 loops on your hook.) Yarn over and draw through all 3 loops on your hook. (You will have 1 loop on your hook when the half double crochet stitch is complete.)

Second Button Tab

With wrong side facing, count 5 stitches from left edge and attach yarn.

Ch 2, hdc to the end.

Repeat rows 23–26.

Middle Button Tab

With wrong side facing, count 5 stitches from the end of the right tab and attach yarn. (If you made a different sized base, you will need to adjust where you start this so it is in the center.)

Ch 2, hdc in the next 5 stitches.

Repeat rows 23–26.

Pockets

Your pocket sizes can also be customized by changing the initial chain count.

Pocket 1 (make 2)

Ch 12.

Row 1: Hdc in 3rd ch from hook and in each stitch across.

Rows 2–6: Ch 2, turn, hdc in each stitch across.

Fasten off, leaving a long tail to sew on pocket.

Pocket 2 (make 2)

Ch 10.

Row 1: Hdc in 3rd ch from hook and in each stitch across.

Rows 2–5: Ch 2, turn, hdc in each stitch across.

Fasten off, leaving a long tail to sew on pocket.

Finishing

Position the pockets where you would like them to be, and sew them on using the long tail and a yarn needle. Place your buttons in the correct position and sew on your 3 buttons as well.

Weave in all ends when done.

Tip: Hang this handy organizer anywhere for easy and convenient storage.

Towel Holder

Skill Level

EASY

Materials

 1 skein separated into 2

Hook: 5 mm/U.S. H-8

Other: 1 button,
yarn needle

Stitches Used

Chain stitch (ch)

Crossed half double crochet (crossed hdc)

Half double crochet (hdc)

Magic circle

Slip stitch (sl st)

Instructions

Hold 2 strands of yarn together to work all stitches for this pattern.

Ring

Make magic circle and ch 2. Work 30 hdc into circle, sl st to first hdc, turn. Pull yarn tail if needed to tighten circle, but don't pull too tight or your stitches will bunch up. Do not fasten off. Continue by adding tab to top of ring.

Tab Top

Row 1: Ch 2 (counts as first hdc), 4 crossed hdc sts in each of the 4 sts across, 1 hdc in last st. Ch 2, turn.

Rows 2–10: Repeat row 1. After 10th row is complete, fasten off and weave in ends.

Fold tab over to top of ring. Position and center button under tab on first row of crossed hdc. Button should fit through the sts in the row. With threaded yarn needle, sew on button. Weave in ends.

Tip: How to make the crossed hdc
Skip 1 stitch, hdc in the next stitch. Go back and hdc in the skipped stitch.

Boot Cuffs

Hook: 6 mm/U.S. J-10
Other: Yarn needle

Skill Level

INTERMEDIATE

Materials

 1 skein

Stitches Used

Chain stitch (ch)
Double crochet (dc)
Single crochet (sc)
Slip stitch (sl st)
Treble crochet (tr)

Instructions

Ribbed Side of Cuff

Ch 13.

Row 1: Dc in 2nd ch st from hook and in each ch st across row. Ch 2, turn.

Row 2: Sc in each st across row. Ch 2, turn.

Row 3: Dc in each st across row, turn.

Repeat rows 2–3 until you reach desired width of the cuff. This piece will need to wrap around your leg in the calf area, so the size will vary depending on the size of your leg.

Once desired width is reached, fold in half and slip stitch together to create a round. Fasten off and weave in ends. Make sure the slip stitched side is on the inside before starting the next step.

Textured Side of Cuff

This part will be worked in rounds on top of the ribbed cuff you just finished.

Round 1: Attach yarn to any st, and evenly sc around the top of the ribbed cuff.

Round 2: Ch 2, *sc in next st, tr in next st; repeat from * around. Sl st to join round.

Round 3: Ch 2, *tr in next st, sc in next st; repeat from * around. Sl st to join round. (Your tr should always be worked into the sc st from the previous round and your sc should always be worked into the tr from the previous round, so adjust your stitches accordingly.)

Continue repeating rounds 2–3 until you reach desired height of boot cuff. Fasten off and weave in ends.

Repeat pattern to make 2nd boot cuff.

Wine Glass Coasters

Skill Level

EASY

Materials

Hook: 3.75 mm/U.S. F-5

Other: Yarn needle

Stitches Used

Chain stitch (ch)
Double crochet (dc)
Magic circle
Single crochet (sc)
Slip stitch (sl st)

Instructions

Bottom

The bottom should measure about 3" when done.

Round 1: Make a magic circle, ch 2, 11 dc into circle, sl st in top ch 2 to join.

Round 2: Ch 2, dc in same st, 2 dc in each st around, sl st in top ch 2 to join.

Round 3: Ch 2, dc in same st, [dc in next st, 2 dc in next st] 11 times, dc, sl st in top ch 2 to join.

Round 4: Ch 1, [2 sc in next st, sc in next 2 sts] 12 times.

Tip: Crocheted coasters in assorted colors are a great way for guests to identify their drinks.

Round 5: Ch 1, sc in back loop only in each st around.

Top

Round 6: Ch 1, *skip 2 sts, 5 dc in next st, skip 2 sts, 1 sc in next st; repeat from * around. Join with a sl st to starting sc.

Round 7: Ch 2, dc in same st. *Skip 2 sts, sl st in next st, skip 2 sts, 3 dc in next st; repeat from * around. 1 dc in same st as first dc. Join with a sl st to first dc.

Fasten off and weave in ends.

Tip: These coasters protect surfaces without falling off the wine glasses.

Camel Stitch Cowl

Skill Level

EASY

Materials

SUPER BULKY

6 2 skeins

Hook: 10 mm/U.S. N-15
Other: Yarn needle

Stitches Used

Camel half double crochet (camel hdc)
Chain stitch (ch)
Half double crochet (hdc)
Slip stitch (sl st)

Tip: Camel hdc stitch

The camel hdc stitch creates a cowl that looks knitted. This stitch is worked like a regular hdc, but instead of into the usual 2 (front and back) loops of a stitch from the previous row or round, the camel hdc is worked into a 3rd loop. The 3rd loop is behind the usual 2 loops. Tip your crochet slightly forward toward you to find the 3rd loop.

Instructions

Ch 60, join with a sl st to first ch to create a round.

Round 1: Ch 2, hdc in each st around, sl st to top of beginning ch 2.

Round 2: Ch 1, camel hdc in each st around, sl st to top of beginning ch 1.

Rounds 3–20 (or desired height): Repeat round 2.

Round 21: Sl st in each st around.

Fasten off and weave in ends.

Half Circle Rug

Skill Level

EASY

Materials

SUPER BULKY

6 skeins (2 of each color)

Hook: 15 mm/U.S. P

Other: Yarn needle

Stitches Used

Chain stitch (ch)

Magic circle

Slip stitch (sl st)

Treble crochet (tr)

Instructions

Hold 3 strands of yarn together to work the pattern.

Row 1: Make a magic circle. Ch 3 (counts as tr here and throughout), 5 tr into circle, turn.

Row 2: Ch 3, tr into same st, 2 tr in each st, turn.

Row 3: Ch 3, tr into same st, tr, *2 tr in next st, tr; rep from * until end of row, turn.

Row 4: Ch 3, tr into same st, tr 2, *2 tr in next st, tr 2; rep from * until end of row, turn.

Row 5: Ch 3, tr into same st, tr 3, *2 tr in next st, tr 3; rep from * until end of row, turn.

Row 6: Ch 3, tr into same st, tr 4, *2 tr in next st, tr 4; rep from * until end of row, turn.

Row 7: Ch 3, tr into same st, tr 5, *2 tr in next st, tr 5; rep from * until end of row, turn.

Row 8: Ch 3, tr into same st, tr 6, *2 tr in next st, tr 6; rep from * until end of row, turn.

Row 9: Ch 3, tr into same st, tr 7, *2 tr in next st, tr 7; rep from * until end of row, turn.

Row 10: Ch 3, tr into same st, tr 8, *2 tr in next st, tr 8; rep from * until end of row, turn.

Row 11: Ch 3, tr into same st, tr 9, *2 tr in next st, tr 9; rep from * until end of row, turn.

Row 12: Ch 3, tr into same st, tr 10, *2 tr in next st, tr 10; rep from * until end of row, turn.

Finishing

Ch 1, sl st across the flat edge of the rug. Fasten off and weave in ends.

Tip: For a larger rug, continue rows in the same manner, increasing the treble crochet in each subsequent row by one. For a smaller rug, stop at any time.

Textured Washcloth

Skill Level

INTERMEDIATE

Materials

 1 skein

Hook: 5 mm/U.S. H-8

Other: Yarn needle

Stitches Used

Back post double crochet (BPdc)

Chain stitch (ch)

Double crochet (dc)

Front post double crochet (FPdc)

Instructions

Ch 32.

Row 1: Dc in 3rd ch from hook (first 3 ch sts count as first dc) and in each ch to end of row, turn.

Row 2: Ch 2 (counts as first st), *FPdc in next 2 sts, BPdc in next 2 sts*; rep from * to * until there is 1 st left, dc in last st. Turn.

Row 3: Ch 2 (counts as first st), FPdc in next st, *BPdc in next 2 sts, FPdc in next 2 sts*; rep from * to * until there are 2 sts left, FPdc in next st, dc in last st. Turn.

Row 4: Ch 2 (counts as first st), *BPdc in next 2 sts, FPdc in next 2 sts*; rep from * to * until there is 1 st left, dc in last st. Turn.

Row 5: Ch 2 (counts as first st), BPdc in next st, *FPdc in next 2 sts, BPdc in next 2 sts*; rep from * to * until there are 2 sts left, BPdc in next st, dc in last st. Turn.

Rep rows 2–5 until you have a square. Fasten off and weave in ends.

Tip: 100% cotton yarn is best for this project because it's washable and holds water well.

Granny Circle Pillow

Skill Level

■ ■ ■ □

INTERMEDIATE

Materials

 MEDIUM 4 5 skeins (1 of each color)

Hook: 5.5 mm / U.S. I-9

Other: 10" round pillow form, yarn needle

Stitches Used

Chain stitch (ch)
Double crochet (dc)
Half double crochet (hdc)
Magic circle
Slip stitch (sl st)

Instructions

Granny Circle (make 1)

With first color, make a magic circle.

Round 1: Ch 3 (counts as dc here and throughout), work 1 dc into circle, ch 2, *2 dc into circle, ch 2; repeat from * 4 more times, join with a sl st in top of beg ch 3. Fasten off.

Round 2: Join 2nd color yarn in any ch-sp. Ch 3, work [1 dc, ch 2, 2 dc] in same ch-sp, ch 2, *[2 dc, ch 2, 2 dc] in next ch-sp, ch 2; repeat from * around, join with a sl st in top of beg ch 3. Fasten off.

Round 3: Join 3rd color yarn in any ch-sp. Ch 3, work 1 dc in same ch-sp, ch 2, *2 dc in next ch-sp, ch 2; repeat from * around, join with a sl st in top of beg ch 3. Fasten off.

Round 4: Join 4th color yarn in any ch-sp. Ch 3, work [1 dc, ch 2, 2 dc] in same ch-sp, ch 2, *[2 dc, ch 2, 2 dc] in next ch-sp, ch 2; repeat from * around, join with a sl st in top of beg ch 3. Fasten off.

Round 5: Join 5th color yarn in any ch-sp. Ch 3, work 1 dc in same ch-sp, ch 2, *2 dc in next ch-sp, ch 2; repeat from * around, join with a sl st in top of beg ch 3. Fasten off.

Round 6: Join first color in any ch-sp. Ch 3, work 1 dc in same ch-sp, ch 2, *2 dc in next ch-sp, ch 2; repeat from * around, join with a sl st in top of beg ch 3. Fasten off.

Round 7: Join 2nd color in any ch-sp. Ch 3, work 1 dc in same ch-sp, ch 2, *2 dc in next ch-sp, ch 2; repeat from * around, join with a sl st in top of beg ch 3. Fasten off.

Round 8: Join 3rd color in any ch-sp. Ch 3, work [1 dc, ch 2, 2 dc] in same ch-sp, ch 2, *[2 dc, ch 2, 2 dc] in next ch-sp, ch 2; repeat from * around, join with a sl st in top of beg ch 3. Fasten off.

Round 9: Join 4th color in any ch-sp. Ch 3, work 1 dc in same ch-sp, ch 2, *2 dc in next ch-sp, ch 2; repeat from * around, join with a sl st in top of beg ch 3. Fasten off.

Plain Circle (make 1)

With first color, make a magic circle.

Round 1: Ch 3 (counts as dc here and throughout), work 9 dc into circle. Join with a sl st in top of beg ch 3. Switch to 2nd color.

Round 2: Ch 3, dc in same st, *dc, 2 dc in next st; repeat from * around. Join with a sl st in top of beg ch 3.

Round 3: Ch 3, dc in same st, *dc in next 2 sts, 2 dc in next st; repeat from * around. Join with a sl st in top of beg ch 3. Switch to 3rd color.

Round 4: Ch 3, dc in same st, *dc in next 3 sts, 2 dc in next st; repeat from * around. Join with a sl st in top of beg ch 3. Switch to 4th color.

Round 5: Ch 3, dc in same st, *dc in next 4 sts, 2 dc in next st; repeat from * around. Join with a sl st in top of beg ch 3. Switch to 5th color.

Round 6: Ch 3, dc in same st, *dc in next 5 sts, 2 dc in next st; repeat from * around. Join with a sl st in top of beg ch 3. Switch to first color.

Round 7: Ch 3, dc in same st, *dc in next 6 sts, 2 dc in next st; repeat from * around. Join with a sl st in top of beg ch 3. Switch to 2nd color.

Round 8: Ch 3, dc in same st, *dc in next 7 sts, 2 dc in next st; repeat from * around. Join with a sl st in top of beg ch 3. Switch to 3rd color.

Round 9: Ch 3, dc in same st, *dc in next 8 sts, 2 dc in next st; repeat from * around. Join with a sl st in top of beg ch 3. Switch to 4th color.

Round 10: Ch 3, dc in same st, *dc in next 9 sts, 2 dc in next st; repeat from * around. Join with a sl st in top of beg ch 3. Fasten off and weave in ends.

Finishing

Make sure all ends are woven in before joining.

Place the granny circle and the plain circle together with wrong sides facing and with the granny circle on top facing you. Using the 5th color and working through both thicknesses, start at any stitch and crochet both circles together using hdc stitches. (Use 1 hdc in all ch-2 spaces of granny circle.)

When you reach the halfway point of joining the circles, insert pillow form between circles. Continue stitching circles together with hdc until completely closed. Fasten off and weave in ends.

Tip: The granny circle and plain circle have a different number of rounds because the stitches in the granny circle make a slightly larger circle.

Garland

Hook: 4 mm/U.S. G-6
Other: Yarn needle

Skill Level

EASY

Materials

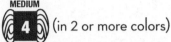 (in 2 or more colors)

Stitches Used

Chain stitch (ch)
Double crochet (dc)
Half double crochet (hdc)
Magic circle
Slip stitch (sl st)

Instructions

With main color, make a magic circle.

Row 1: Hdc 4 in the circle. Pull circle tight, but do not close ring. Leave as a half circle. Ch 1, turn.

Row 2: 2 hdc in each st across row. Ch 1, turn.

Row 3: *Hdc in next st, 2 hdc in next st; rep from * across row. Ch 1, turn.

Row 4: *Hdc in next 2 sts, 2 hdc in next st; rep from * across row. Ch 1, turn.

Row 5: *Hdc in next 3 sts, 2 hdc in next st; rep from * across row. Turn.

Switch to contrast color for next row.

Row 6: Ch 2, 2 dc in same st, *sk 1 st, sl st into next st, sk 1 st, 5 dc in next st; rep from * across row until last 3 sts. Sk 1 st. Sl st into next st. 2 dc in last st. Fasten off and weave in ends. Rep pattern to make desired number of half circles, changing contrast colors as needed.

Finishing
Once you have desired number of half circles for garland, arrange and order them in a line. With long strand of yarn and yarn needle, evenly st half circles tog, leaving an equal length of yarn bet them.

Pyramid Potpourri Sachet

Skill Level

INTERMEDIATE

Materials

MEDIUM
4 (in 3 colors)

Hook: 5.5 mm/U.S. I-9

Other: Polyfill stuffing, potpourri, yarn needle

Stitches Used

Chain stitch (ch)
Magic circle
Single crochet (sc)
Slip stitch (sl st)

Instructions

This pattern is made by making 4 triangles that will be joined together to create a pyramid.

Triangle (make 4)

With the first color, make a magic circle.

Round 1: Continuing with the first color, work into the circle [sc, ch 1, sc, ch 3] 3 times. Join with a sl st to the first sc, fasten off.

Round 2: Join 2nd color into the middle of any ch-3 corner sp. Sc, ch 1, sc in space, *ch 1, sc in next ch-1 sp, ch 1, **(sc, ch 1, sc, ch 2, sc, ch 1, sc)*** in next ch-3 corner sp. Rep from * to ** once and from * to *** once. Finish with (sc, ch 1, sc) in beginning ch-3 corner sp. Ch 2, join with a sl st to first sc, fasten off.

Round 3: Join first color into the middle of any ch-2 corner sp. Sc in sp, *[ch 1, sc in ch-1 sp] 4 times, ch 1, **(sc, ch 3, sc) in ch-2 corner sp*. Rep from * to * once and from * to ** once. Finish with sc in same sp as first sc, ch 3, join with a sl st to first st, fasten off.

Round 4: Join 3rd color into the middle of any ch-3 corner sp. Sc, ch 1, sc in sp, *[ch 1, sc in ch-1 sp] 5 times, ch 1, **(sc, ch 1, sc, ch 2, sc, ch 1, sc) in ch-3 corner sp*. Rep from * to * once and from * to ** once. Finish with (sc, ch 1, sc) in beginning ch-3 corner sp, ch 2, join with a sl st to first sc, fasten off and weave in all ends.

Finishing

Using the first color, start with holding two triangles together and sc evenly through both along one edge. Continue working around with rows of sc to join all triangles together to create a pyramid. Before closing the final edge, stuff pyramid with polyfill stuffing and potpourri. Close final edge. Fasten off and weave in all ends.

Hanging Loop (optional)

Attach yarn to top of the pyramid and ch 8 (or desired size of loop). Sl st to beginning ch and fasten off.

Ear Warmer

Other: Yarn needle

Skill Level

EXPERIENCED

Materials

MEDIUM
4

Hook: 5 mm/U.S. H-8

Stitches Used

Back post double crochet (BPdc)

Chain stitch (ch)

Double crochet (dc)

Front post double crochet (FPdc)

Single crochet (sc)

Slip stitch (sl st)

Instructions

Ch 15.

Row 1: Dc in 3rd ch from hook and in each ch across. Ch 2, turn.

Row 2: Sk first st, FPdc around next st, dc in next 2 sts, FPdc around next 6 sts, dc in next 2 sts, FPdc around next st, dc in last st. Ch 2, turn.

Row 3: Sk first st, BPdc around next st, dc in next 2 sts, BPdc around next 6 sts, dc in next 2 sts, BPdc around next st, dc in last st. Ch 2, turn.

Row 4: Sk first st, FPdc around next st, dc in next 2 sts, sk 3 sts, FPdc around next 3 sts. FPdc around first skipped st, FPdc around 2nd skipped st, FPdc around 3rd skipped st. Dc in next 2 sts, FPdc around next st, dc in last st. Ch 2, turn.

Row 5: Sk first st, BPdc around next st, dc in next 2 sts, BPdc around next 6 sts, dc in next 2 sts, BPdc around next st, dc in last st. Ch 2, turn.

Row 6: Sk first st, FPdc around next st, dc in next 2 sts, FPdc around next 6 sts, dc in next 2 sts, FPdc around next st, dc in last st. Ch 2, turn.

Row 7: Sk first st, BPdc around next st, dc in next 2 sts, BPdc around next 6 sts, dc in next 2 sts, BPdc around next st, dc in last st. Ch 2, turn.

Row 8: Sk first st, FPdc around next st, dc in next 2 sts, sk 3 sts, FPdc around next 3 sts. FPdc around first skipped st, FPdc around 2nd skipped st, FPdc around 3rd skipped st. Dc in next 2 sts, FPdc around next st, dc in last st. Ch 2, turn.

Repeat rows 5–8 until you reach desired length (typical sizing will be about 20–21"). Fasten off and weave in ends. Hold ends of ear warmer together. Attach new yarn and sl st ends together, making sure to sl st along the wrong side (the side that will face in).

Edging

Ch 1, work 2 sc over each dc and 1 sc over each ch 2. Join. Ch 1, sc in same st and in each st around. Fasten off.

Now join with a sl st to the opposite side of ear warmer: Ch 1, work 2 sc over each dc and 1 sc over each ch 2. Join. Ch 1, sc in same st and in each st around. Fasten off and weave in ends.

Door Draft Stopper

Skill Level

INTERMEDIATE

Materials

 5 skeins

Hook: 6.5 mm/U.S. K-10.5

Other: Stuffing, yarn needle

Stitches Used

Chain stitch (ch)

Double crochet (dc)

Magic circle

Scale stitch

Single crochet (sc)

Slip stitch (sl st)

Tip: Scale stitch

The scale stitch is worked around 2 dc posts. It starts with 5 dc stitches around and down the first post, then ch 1, and work 5 dc stitches around and up the 2nd dc post.

Instructions

Make a magic circle.

Round 1: 6 sc into circle.

Round 2: 2 sc in each st around.

Round 3: *2 sc in next st, sc in next st; repeat from * around.

Round 4: *2 sc in next st, sc in next 2 sts; repeat from * around.

Round 5: *2 sc in next st, sc in next 3 sts; repeat from * around.

Round 6: *2 sc in next st, sc in next 4 sts; repeat from * around.

Round 7: Ch 2, dc in same st, *ch 2, sk 2 sts, 2 dc in next st; repeat from * around. Join with a sl st between beginning ch 2 and dc.

Round 8: *Ch 1, sk next 2 dc pair and scale st around next 2 dc pair. Repeat from * around. You should have 6 scales. Join with a sl st in beginning dc of first scale.

Round 9: Sl st into space between sts below. Ch 2, dc into space between sts below where you just sl stitched. *Ch 2, 2 dc in center space of scale, ch 2, 2 dc in between the next 2 dc and around the ch 1 between the scales. Rep from * around. End with a sl st between the first ch 2 and dc.

Repeat rounds 8–9 until desired length (long enough for doorway or window). The scale stitches should be staggered. Once desired length is reached, fasten off and weave in ends.

Fill with chosen stuffing material. Polyfill stuffing works well, as do old T-shirts, rags, or socks. If possible, use stuffing similar in color to your yarn to prevent the stuffing from showing through the scales.

End Cap

Make a magic circle.

Round 1: 6 sc into circle.

Round 2: 2 sc in each st around.

Round 3: *2 sc in next st, sc in next st; repeat from * around.

Round 4: *2 sc in next st, sc in next 2 sts; repeat from * around.

Round 5: *2 sc in next st, sc in next 3 sts; repeat from * around.

Round 6: *2 sc in next st, sc in next 4 sts; repeat from * around.

Fasten off, leaving a long tail for sewing.

Sew this circle onto the open end of the door draft stopper. Weave in all ends.

Mop Cover

Skill Level

EASY

Materials

 100% cotton

Hook: 5 mm/U.S. H-8

Other: Yarn needle

Stitches Used

Chain stitch (ch)
Crossed half double crochet (crossed hdc)
Half double crochet (hdc)
Single crochet (sc)
Single crochet 3 together (sc3tog)
Slip stitch (sl st)

Instructions

This pattern fits a 10" x 4" mop, but can be adjusted to any size by increasing or decreasing the number of chains.

Ch 35.

Row 1: Hdc in 2nd ch from hook, crossed hdc across row until last ch, hdc in last ch. Ch 1, turn.

Row 2: Working in front loops only, sc in first st and in each st across. Ch 1, turn.

Row 3: Hdc in first st, crossed hdc across row until last ch, hdc in last ch. Ch 1, turn.

Rows 4–9: Repeat rows 2 and 3.

Tip: It's important to use 100% cotton yarn for washability and cleaning purposes.

Edging

Choose which side you would like facing, face that side toward you and begin working in rounds.

Round 1: Ch 1, sc around with 1 sc in each st and evenly spaced sc along each short side; join with a sl st in first sc. Note: Do not increase at corners.

Rounds 2–3: Ch 1, sc in each st around; join with a sl st in first sc.

Rounds 4–7: Ch 1, sc around, working 1 sc3tog in each corner. Join with a sl st in first sc.

Fasten off and weave in ends.

Tip: How to make the crossed hdc
Skip 1 stitch, hdc in next stitch. Go back and hdc in the skipped stitch.

Reversible Placemat

Skill Level

EXPERIENCED

Materials

 MEDIUM 4 2 skeins (1 of each color)

Hook: 5.5 mm/U.S. I-9
Other: Yarn needle

Stitches Used

Back double crochet (back dc)

Chain stitch (ch)

Double crochet (dc)

Front double crochet (front dc)

Half double crochet (hdc)

Magic circle

Single crochet (sc)

Slip stitch (sl st)

Tip: Front dc

If the layer you are working on is in back of the previous layer, you will work your dc through the other layer to interlock both layers together. If your layer is already in front of the previous layer, you will work your dc normally.

Tip: Back dc

If the layer you are working on is in front of the previous layer, you will work your dc through the other layer to interlock both layers together. If your layer is already in back of the previous layer, you will work your dc normally.

Instructions

This technique is called interlocking crochet, and you will be working with two layers at the same time, joining them together with certain stitches as you work.

A. With main color (here white), ch 52, dc in 6th ch from hook, [ch 1, sk next ch, dc in next ch] across; *(24 boxes)*

B. With 2nd color (here blue), ch 50, dc in 6th ch from hook, [ch 1, sk next ch, dc in next ch] across. *(23 boxes)*

Row 1:

Place main color layer on top of 2nd color layer, with working yarn of both pieces at the same, right edge.

A. With main color, ch 4, front dc in next dc, *ch 1, back dc in next dc, [ch 1, front dc in next dc] 3 times; rep from * across to last 3 dc, ch 1, back dc in next dc, [ch 1, front dc in next dc] twice;

B. With 2nd color, ch 4, front dc in next dc, ch 1, front dc in next st, *[ch 1, back dc in next dc] twice, [ch 1, front dc in next dc] twice; rep from * across to last dc, ch 1, back dc in last dc, turn.

Row 2:

A. With main color, ch 4, back dc in next dc, *ch 1, front dc in next dc, [ch 1, back dc in next dc] 3 times; rep from * across to last 3 dc, ch 1, front dc in next dc, [ch 1, back dc in next dc] twice;

B. With 2nd color, ch 4, front dc in next dc, [ch 1, front dc in next dc] across, turn.

Row 3:

A. With main color, ch 4, front dc in next dc, [ch 1, front dc in next dc] twice, *ch 1, back dc in next dc, [ch 1, front dc in next dc] 3 times; rep from * across to last dc, ch 1, front dc in last st;

B. With 2nd color, ch 4, back dc in next dc, ch 1, back dc in next dc, *[ch 1, front dc in next dc] twice, [ch 1, back dc in next dc] twice; rep from * across to last dc, ch 1, back dc in last st, turn.

Row 4:

A. With main color, ch 4, back dc in next dc, [ch 1, back dc in next dc] twice, *ch 1, front dc in next dc, [ch 1, back dc in next dc] 3 times; rep from * across to last dc, ch 1, back dc in last dc;

B. With 2nd color, ch 4, front dc in next dc, [ch 1, front dc in next dc] across, turn.

Next rows: [Rep rows 1–4] until desired size, then rep rows 1 and 2 once.

Next row: With main color, ch 4, front dc in next dc, [ch 1, front dc in next dc] across, turn.

2nd Color Edging
This edging is worked around the edge of the 2nd color layer only.

Evenly sp hdc around all edges, working 1 hdc in each st and in each box with 3 hdc in each corner, sl st in first hdc, fasten off and weave in ends.

Main Color Edging

This edging is worked around the edge of the main color layer only.

Evenly sp sc around all edges with 1 sc in each st and in each box with 3 sc in each corner, join with a sl st in first sc, do not fasten off.

Final Edging

There are more sts in main color edging than in 2nd color edging, so, to ensure an even edging, occasionally work 2 sc in the same st of 2nd color edging but in different sts of main color edging.

With main color, work through both thicknesses in back loops only and sc in each st around with 3 sc in center corner st, join with a sl st in first sc.

Fasten off and weave in all ends.

Tip: This placemat is almost 19.5" wide and about 13" high when complete.